P9-DFW-579

OCT - - 2008

Heroes

Craig Kielburger

Free The Children

Rachel Lynette

KIDHAVEN PRESS
A part of Gale, Cengage Learning

GALE
CENGAGE Learning™

Detroit • New York • San Francisco • New Haven, Conn • Waterville, Maine • London

ST. THOMAS PUBLIC LIBRA

GALE
CENGAGE Learning™

© 2008 Gale, Cengage Learning

ALL RIGHTS RESERVED. No part of this work covered by the copyright herein may be reproduced, transmitted, stored, or used in any form or by any means graphic, electronic, or mechanical, including but not limited to photocopying, recording, scanning, digitizing, taping, Web distribution, information networks, or information storage and retrieval systems, except as permitted under Section 107 or 108 of the 1976 United States Copyright Act, without the prior written permission of the publisher.

Every effort has been made to trace the owners of copyrighted material.

LIBRARY OF CONGRESS CATALOGING-IN-PUBLICATION DATA

Lynette, Rachel.
  Craig Kielburger : Free the Children / by Rachel Lynette.
    p. cm. — (Young heroes)
  Includes bibliographical references and index.
  ISBN 978-0-7377-4050-9 (hardcover)
  1. Kielburger, Craig. 2. Social reformers—Canada—Biography. 3. Child labor.
  4. Children's rights. 5. Free the Children (Organization) I. Title.
  HD6231.L96 2008
  331.3'1092—dc22
  [B]
                                                                    2008003550

KidHaven Press
27500 Drake Rd
Farmington Hills MI 48331

ISBN-13: 978-0-7377-4050-9
ISBN-10: 0-7377-4050-7

Printed in the United States of America
1 2 3 4 5 6 7 12 11 10 09 08

Contents

Introduction

Kids Saving Kids

When Craig Kielburger was twelve years old, he read an article that changed his life and eventually those of millions of others around the world. The article was about the murder of a Pakistani youth labor **activist**, and it inspired Craig to start Free The Children. Free The Children is a **nonprofit organization** with the mission of freeing children from abuse, exploitation, and also to free young people from the idea that they are powerless to create positive social change. There are over 218 million child laborers in **developing countries** throughout the world. Instead of going to school, these children work long hours for little or no money.

In order to learn everything he could about child labor, Craig traveled to some of the poorest areas in the world. He met children who worked in factories making carpets and fireworks. These children inspired Craig to let the world know about child labor.

Craig started Free The Children when he was twelve years old.

Today, Free The Children is the largest network of children helping children. Through the work and donations of its members, Free The Children improves the lives of children living in developing countries by building schools, providing access to clean water and health care, and helping families to earn money to live above **poverty**.

One

Inspired to Help

Craig Kielburger was born on December 17, 1982, in Thornhill, a small town near the city of Toronto in Ontario, Canada. Craig's parents, Fred and Theresa Kielburger are both teachers. Craig also has an older brother, Marc.

As a young child, Craig was involved in Boy Scouts and enjoyed camping, sports, reading, and spending time with his brother. Unfortunately, he suffered from ear infections that caused partial hearing loss. This resulted in Craig not hearing words correctly, so he did not pronounce them properly. Craig overcame this with the help of a speech therapist. By the time he was ten years old, he was no longer getting ear infections.

When he was eleven, Craig entered a public speaking competition. Although he had prepared a speech, when he got to the podium, he completely forgot it. Instead, he told the audience about his own personal experiences. "I began speaking from my heart about the things I had learned about winning,"[1] said Craig. Craig won the competition and went on to win four more, taking second place in the final competition.

An Ordinary Morning

In April 1995, a year after the speech competition, when Craig was twelve years old, he came across a disturbing story in the *Toronto Star* newspaper. It was about a twelve-year-old youth activist from Pakistan named Iqbal Masih. Iqbal had spent most of his life as a child slave, chained to a loom. A loom is a frame that is used to make rugs. When Iqbal was freed, he got involved in the movement to end child labor. Iqbal was shot and killed while riding his bicycle because of his involvement.

Craig could not stop thinking about Iqbal. "What struck me most . . . was the similarity in our ages and the

The story of Iqbal Masih, center, inspired Craig to start Free The Children.

Reebok Human Rights Award

massive difference in our lives,"[2] said Craig. Craig spent the next few days learning everything he could about child labor. He did research at the library and called human rights organizations. He learned that children in many developing countries work for long hours in often dangerous conditions for little or even no pay. Craig could not believe that millions of children younger than he was were treated so horribly. Craig felt he had to do something to help them.

A Plea for Help

Craig decided to start a children's group to help child laborers. He began by speaking to his seventh grade class. Craig made copies of the newspaper story about Iqbal and passed them out to his classmates. "As I spoke I could see that many of my classmates were just as shocked as I was by the story,"[3] said Craig.

One of Craig's goals was to increase awareness about child labor. He did so by speaking to his classmates and inspiring them to get involved.

That afternoon, Craig and eleven of his classmates met as his house. They decided that their first goal was to inform people about child labor. They came up with the name "Free The Children." They also decided to participate in a youth fair in Toronto. They made a display with information about child labor.

At the fair, Craig noticed that the other groups had very professional-looking displays with videos, books, and brochures. Even though their display was simple, Free The Children got a great deal of attention. The other presenters were all adults helping children. Free The Children was the only group made up of children who wanted to help other children. "That day our second goal emerged," said Craig. "Putting more power in the hands of children. Children needed to have a voice and participate in issues that affect them."[4]

Spreading the Word

Free The Children set up an office in the Kielburger family den. They put together packets of information on child labor and sent them out to groups and schools. Eventually, they were asked to speak at a nearby school.

Craig and two other members of Free The Children spoke to four classes. They told the stories of child laborers and challenged the students to take action by writing letters. They suggested that they write to companies, urging them not to sell products made with child labor, and to leaders of developing countries, asking them to protect children. The presentations all went well, and when they finished the last one, they were

Craig and other Free The Children members spoke to classrooms, gave presentations, and encouraged children to write letters.

presented with a stack of letters from the first class they had visited.

That first request to speak at the school was followed by many more. Free The Children established a reputation of giving interesting and informative presentations. When students asked questions they could not answer, Free The Children members researched the answers and learned even more about child labor.

Taking Action

Summer break meant no more classroom presentations, but that did not stop Free The Children from taking action. They had heard that an East Indian child activist named Kailash Satyarthi had been put in jail by his government. Free The Children wrote letters to the **prime minister** of India and organized a **petition** demanding Satyarthi's release. Over 3,000 people signed the petition. Free The Children put the petition and the letters into a shoebox and sent it to the Indian government. Satyarthi was freed, and he later said that the shoebox was one of the most powerful things anyone had ever done for him.

Free The Children also held a fundraising garage sale over the summer to raise money for educational materials and other Free The Children expenses. By now, the group had grown to over 50 members. The event was much more than a garage sale. They also sold handmade jewelry and lemonade. Kids dressed up like clowns to entertain small children while parents shopped. Throughout the sale Free The Children members took the opportunity to tell their customers about their cause.

Free The Children took action by organizing a petition demanding the release of East Indian child activist Kailash Satyarthi.

Making Headlines

In the fall of 1995, Craig was asked to speak to the delegates of the Ontario Federation of Labour (OFL). The OFL is an organization dedicated to making sure workers are treated fairly. Although he was one of many speakers, Craig was allowed to speak for much longer than his allotted time. When he was done, he received a **standing ovation**. After the applause died down, the leader of the OFL **pledged** 5,000 dollars to Free The Children. Immediately, the leader of another union of laborers pledged a donation. One by one, other unions pledged money to Free The Children—the autoworkers' union, the steelworkers' union, and many more. By the end of the evening, Free The Children had 150,000 dollars in pledges!

The next morning the front page of the *Toronto Star* read, "Boy, 12, Takes OFL by Storm with Child Labour Plea." The picture showed Craig and other Free The Children members holding up a petition with thousands of signatures.

Trip to Asia

Craig was thrilled that Free The Children was growing so

Free The Children earned 150,000 dollars in pledges after Craig spoke to the Ontario Federation of Labour.

fast. But he felt that to truly understand the issue of child labor, he had to see it for himself and actually meet working children. Craig got his opportunity when 24-year-old activist Alam Raham asked him to come with him on a trip to South Asia. Alam was part of an organization called Youth Action Network. Alam had been encouraging Craig since Free The Children began and Alam had become a friend and a mentor.

Although Craig's parents admired and trusted Alam, they were still uneasy about sending their twelve-year-old son to some of poorest regions in the world. They set two conditions for the trip. First, Craig had to convince them that he would be safe, and, second, he had to raise half the money for the plane fare himself. To convince his parents he would be safe, Craig worked with humanitarian agencies that had similar goals to Free The Children's. These agencies were located in Asia and were able to find Craig lodging and transportation in the countries he would visit. Alam answered as many of his parent's questions as he could. Craig raised money by doing chores for family and neighbors, selling hockey cards, and hinting to his relatives that money toward the trip would make a great early birthday gift. Eventually, his parents agreed to let him go.

Chapter Two

Off to Asia

The three-week trip to Asia was originally planned for Craig's winter break so that he would miss only a week of school. But Craig soon realized that three weeks was not long enough and the trip grew to seven weeks. On December 9, 1995, Craig started his journey to Dhaka, Bangladesh, where Alam, who had gone on ahead, met him at the airport.

Working Children

Together, Craig and Alam traveled to Thailand, India, Nepal, and Pakistan. They saw people living in crowded **slums** with no electricity or running water. "The people who lived there owned next to nothing. Their clothing was in rags. Human and animal waste filled the gutters,"[5] said Craig. Craig also met many working children.

The children he met worked in factories, shops, mines, quarries, and alleys. Some children worked in their family businesses doing things like working in a tea shop or selling produce. Some children worked for other people and used their small earnings to help their families. There were even children who were sold as slaves by their own parents. In some places, entire families worked for one person because a parent or a grandparent had borrowed

In 1995, Craig traveled to Asia where he met many working children.

money from that person. The family worked to repay the debt, but because they were overcharged for their food and every mistake they made, it was impossible to ever pay the debt off.

One of the most disturbing situations that Craig saw involved a young Indian girl named Muniannal. Her job was to take apart and sort used **syringes** so the parts could be resold. The syringes were heaped in a pile in front of her, many of them dirty and caked with dried blood. The job was very dangerous because the syringes could carry diseases like HIV and hepatitis. Muniannal was barefoot and wore no protective clothing. She worked for eleven hours a day and was paid less than 2 cents an hour.

Another sad situation that Craig learned about was of a boy from Nepal who was sold into slavery by his parents. He was forced to work in a tea shop washing teacups. If he broke a cup, the owner would yell at him and beat him. He tried to escape many times, but each time, he was caught and beaten. Eventually, he got very sick and the owner dumped him in the street. An aid worker found him and took him to a hospital where he recovered. When Craig met the boy, he was about eight years old and living in a halfway house. A halfway house is a safe place for children to recover until they can go home or live on their own.

Working for Change

In addition to meeting children in Asia, Craig also met with human rights organizations that were working to

In Asia, in addition to meeting children Craig also met with members of human rights organizations.

make positive change. He learned about programs that were helping working children and met the workers who devoted their lives to the children.

He met teachers who brought education to child workers by teaching them where they worked. The children were given a few hours off to attend the classes that met on docks, under trees, or in empty sheds. He met people who worked to help the families of children who were hurt in explosions at fireworks factories. They wanted the factory owners to give money to families when a child was hurt or killed. He met people who ran halfway houses and who helped children who were living on the streets by giving them food, clothing, and a place to sleep. He also met people who were working to change child labor laws by **lobbying** officials and holding public marches to protest child labor.

Meeting Mother Teresa

Craig also met one of the most famous humanitarians in the world: Mother Teresa. Craig had always admired Mother Teresa for her work with some of the world's most needy people. Mother Teresa held Craig's hands in hers as he told her about Free The Children. He asked her to pray for the child laborers. She blessed him and promised to pray for the children. Mother Teresa also gave Craig three religious medals.

Craig's visit with Mother Teresa had a strong effect. "As we left the convent, the dismal streets took on a different, almost hopeful light," said Craig. "Mother Teresa's message of steady and unyielding compassion seemed to open up a path through the poverty and sickness that characterized so much of the city."[6]

Freeing the Children

Craig was glad for Mother Teresa's prayers when they got to Varanasi, India, where Alam, along with other activists, took part in a police raid on a carpet factory. The activists took the factory by surprise and were able to free all of the 22 boys who lived and worked there. The boys had worked, eaten, and slept on the dirt floors next to the looms where they tied thousands of tiny knots to make the carpets. Children who cried or fell asleep at the loom were beaten or burned with cigarettes.

Craig was not allowed to go on the raid, but he did go on the trip to take the boys back to their families. The boys' parents had been lied to and told that their sons would attend school and learn carpet weaving in their spare time while being paid a good wage.

It took eleven hours to get to the boys' village. They arrived in the middle of the night. Each boy was taken to his house and reunited with his family. Craig describes what happened when eight-year-old Munnilal returned home:

> An old man appeared. In the moonlight he called out excitedly, "Everyone, wake up! Come quick! It's Munnilal!"
>
> Soon, the whole family emerged. "Munnilal, is it really you?" cried out his tearful mother. She touched his face, and pulled him tightly to her. They stood there motionless, as if the world had stopped.[7]

World Trade and Child Labor

After the carpet factory raid, Craig and Alam traveled to Delhi, India, where they toured a **rehabilitation center** for children who had been slaves. There Craig met a boy named Nagashir who had worked in a carpet factory for seven years. He showed Craig his arms, legs, and throat where he had been branded with a hot iron for trying to help his younger brother escape. Nagashir's story inspired Craig to hold a **press conference.** "I believed that telling this one story would create such outrage people would immediately demand an end to child labour,"[8] said Craig.

At that time, there were a lot of reporters from the Canadian media in Delhi because the Canadian prime minister, Jean Chrétien, had just been there as part of a tour of Asia to promote world trade. Craig had been disappointed to hear that the child labor issue was not on Chrétien's agenda. Craig hoped the press conference would bring the issue to Chrétien's attention.

Craig insisted that all the speakers be children, saying, "Who can better understand and sympathize with children than children themselves?"[9] Craig spoke at the press conference as a representative of Canada, and Asmita, the ten-year-old daughter of the head of the South Asian Coalition Against Child Servitude also spoke. But by far the most effective speakers were Nagashir and another boy named Mohan, who had also worked in a carpet factory. As the boys described how they had been treated, Craig could see the shock and sadness on the reporters' faces.

Craig held a press conference in Delhi, India, and spoke, along with other children, about child labor issues.

The story hit the news the next day. It was on all the TV news networks, including CNN. The media wanted to know why child labor was not on the prime minister's agenda. Because of these questions, Chrétien agreed to see Craig for a short meeting. During the meeting, Chrétien agreed to talk about the child labor issue with Asian governments.

Back to Canada

Craig had seen and accomplished a great deal during his seven weeks in Asia. But to him, the time he spent with the children was more important than meeting Mother Teresa and Prime Minister Chrétien. "It is the children I've met who are my real heroes,"[10] says Craig. Throughout his trip, he had met children living in terrible situations who shared what little they had and treated others with kindness. Even though he was returning home, he knew he would never forget the faces and the stories of children whose childhoods were spent in forced labor instead of playing and learning.

Chapter Three

Free The Children in Action

Craig's return to Canada was a triumphant one. He was met at the airport not only by his family, but also by his friends in Free The Children, his Boy Scout troupe, and many reporters. Craig's story had caught the attention of the media and over the next few weeks he was interviewed for magazine and newspaper articles and appeared on several American TV shows, including *Good Morning America* and *60 Minutes*.

Working for Free The Children

Even though he was only thirteen years old, Craig had earned a reputation as an expert on child labor and had become a popular speaker. In April 1996 he was invited to Washington, D.C., where he met with then vice president Al Gore and his family. He also testified at the Democratic Policy Committee hearing on Consumer Choice and Corporate Responsibility. He urged the committee to take action to stop child labor. Among other things, he asked that corporations that take advantage of inexpensive labor in developing countries make sure they are not using child labor. He also called for a labeling system that would identify products made by children so that consumers could choose not to buy

Craig's reputation grew quickly, and, in 1996, he met with then vice president Al Gore and his family.

those products. Craig told the committee about Free The Children and ended his presentation saying:

> Some people are surprised at what we are doing. But the real heroes are the boys and girls who work in slave-like conditions to make soccer balls which your children play with, to make clothes which your children wear, to even make fireworks which light up the American skies on the 4th of July. You are a powerful nation. You have the power in your words, in your actions, and in your policy making to give these children hope for a better life. What will you do to help these children?[11]

In addition to school and his work with Free The Children, Craig also found time to work with author Kevin Major to write a book about his trip to Asia. *Free the Children: A Young Man's Personal Crusade Against Child Labor* was published in 1998. The book won the Christopher Award for spreading a message of hope and understanding.

The book, as well as Craig's many speaking engagements, was bringing attention to Free The Children, and the organization was growing fast. Free The Children groups were sprouting up all over North America. By 1999 Free The Children had over 100,000 members.

Leaders Today

Craig was excited that so many children wanted to get involved in Free The Children. But he soon found that although children wanted to help, they were often frus-

Craig and his brother, Marc, founded Leaders Today, which helps children increase their skills in public speaking, negotiating, and fundraising.

trated because they did not know how to get adults to take them seriously. According to the Leaders Today Web site, "Calls and letters poured in from discouraged youth who wanted to make a difference, but didn't know where to start. Others came from disheartened youth who had tried to start campaigns only to be told to wait until they were older and more experienced."[12]

Craig knew that children could make a powerful impact if they just had the tools that they needed. To give young people these tools, Craig and his brother, Marc, founded Leaders Today in 1999. They developed classes on public speaking, **negotiating**, and fundraising.

Within a few years Leaders Today teachers were giving classes throughout North America. Leaders Today also organizes youth volunteer trips to developing countries.

Awards and Accomplishments

Through his work with Free The Children and Leaders Today, Craig has been able to travel to over 50 countries. He has met many famous people, spoken to government officials, and been invited to consult with the United Nations. Craig has also received many awards for his accomplishments.

One of the first awards was the Reebok Youth in Action Award, which he received in 1996. This award was especially meaningful to Craig because Iqbal Masih, the Pakistani youth activist, had received the same award just two years earlier. Craig has received many other awards, including the Roosevelt Freedom Medal in 1998 and the Nelson Mandela Human Rights Award in 2003. He has been nominated for the Nobel Peace Prize four times, and he has received four **honorary doctorates.** In 2007 Free The Children won the Skoll Foundation Award. This award comes with a grant of over a million dollars to help Free The Children reach its goals.

Free The Children Programs

Over the years, Free The Children has organized many campaigns and programs. At first, most of these programs were direct efforts to help end child labor. Members held letter-writing and petition drives. They held fundraisers and worked to raise awareness about the issue. However, Free The Children members soon realized that the problem of child labor cannot be solved simply by making it against the law. Governments and aid groups must offer alternatives to people living in developing countries. Adults need ways to make a living so that they do not have to depend on their children's wages. Children need to attend school so they will have more opportunities as adults.

The work of Free The Children supports the idea that "education is the best way to break the cycle of poverty and end the exploitation of children."[13] They build schools and provide teachers and resources. So far, Free The Children has built over 500 primary schools in sixteen developing countries. These schools serve over 50,000 children every day. In addition to building schools, Free The Children also sends thousands of school supply kits each year.

Changing Lives

Even if there is a school nearby, many children in developing countries cannot attend because their families need the money they can make by working. To help solve this problem, Free The Children has programs that help parents to make enough money to support their families. They do this by giving the parents the tools they need to make money. For some families, this might be a piece of land to farm. For other families a single milking cow can make the difference between poverty and a decent living. Other families are given a

Believing that education is essential, Free The Children also builds schools in developing countries and provides teachers and resources.

sewing machine and taught to mend and sew. Free The Children also offers training so the parents can learn to use the equipment and market their skills. Free The Children has helped over 23,500 families.

Another big problem for people in developing counties is illness. Diseases like typhoid, cholera, and malaria not only claim lives, but they also keep children from school and parents from work. Also, families often cannot afford treatment or the cost of traveling to the hospital. Free The Children helps families by building community health clinics and training people in the community to be health-care workers. They also make sure the clinics have medical equipment and supplies. These clinics have made a huge difference in the lives of over 512,500 people in developing countries.

Free The Children has changed many lives. But Craig believes that one of Free The Children's greatest accomplishments is proving to the world that young people can make a difference.

Four

What You Can Do

E ven though Craig is no longer a child, he still believes that children have the power to change the world. Free The Children has grown into the world's largest network of children helping children. Over a million children in 45 countries help support Free The Children. There are many ways that young people can get involved in Free The Children.

Start a Youth in Action Group

One of the most helpful things kids can do is start a Youth in Action group. A Youth in Action group is a group of young people who are committed to taking social action. Free The Children offers a great deal of support for Youth in Action groups. On the Free The Children Web site there are step-by-step instructions on how to start a group. Free The Children also offers live support. Each Youth in Action group has a contact at Free The Children who can answer questions and make suggestions. In addition, the Free The Children Web site offers ways for Youth in Action groups to connect with each other. There are Youth in Action blogs, Web pages, a Free The Children newsletter, and a We Generation Zone on Free The Children's Web site that allows youths to connect with other youths and to get the resources they need to make a difference.

One way that children can get involved with Free The Children is by starting a Youth in Action group.

Pick a Program

Free The Children has several programs or campaigns that people of all ages can support. There are many ways to get involved. Free The Children supplies kits for each campaign with detailed how-to guides, informational brochures, fundraising ideas, and colorful posters.

Many of Free The Children's causes are supported by the Adopt-a-Village campaign. This campaign helps

The Vow of Silence is a successful Free The Children campaign that raises money and awareness.

to build healthy communities by building schools, providing health care, improving water and sanitation, and providing ways for parents to make enough money to support their families so that children have the freedom to go to school.

For this program, individuals or groups choose one component each year to focus on. Free The Children has a program for each component. For example, for the Brick by Brick school building program, participants build a school by placing paper bricks on a large poster of a school. Each brick represents a sum of money that they have raised. When the poster is complete, the group has raised enough money to build a real school.

Halloween for Hunger is another program that young people can participate in to help underprivileged children in their own communities. In this program, young people collect nonperishable food items on Halloween instead of candy. They can then give the food they collect to their local food bank. Trick-or-treating for food also sends a powerful message. According to the Free The Children Web site, "By participating in Halloween for Hunger, you and your team can make a real difference in the lives of those living with hunger in your community."[14]

Another successful campaign is the Vow of Silence. The Vow of Silence campaign raises awareness and funds by having participants remain silent to honor those children whose voices are not heard. The first part of the campaign is not silent. During this time, participants talk to people about the problem of child labor and collect pledges. Then, at midnight on March 1, participants join together and begin their vow of silence.

Young people who do not want to make a vow of silence might find the Celebrate for Change campaign more appealing. For this campaign, children hold a birthday party in honor of the millions of children around the world who do not know the date of their own birthdays. Children can dedicate their own birthday parties to this cause, or throw a different party. Guests are asked to bring donations instead of presents.

Make Some Money

Free The Children could not do its work without donations from its members. Although Free The Children also receives money from adults and corporations, over 60 percent of the money they receive comes from kids. The Free The Children Web site offers a fundraising guide with ideas for individuals, groups, and even whole schools and communities.

Young people can provide a service, like walking dogs or mowing lawns. They can make things to sell, like jewelry, artwork, or a collection of recipes. Garage sales and bake sales are another good way to make money. Free The Children also suggests that young people can "Party for a Cause" by hosting an event like a game night or karaoke party, and then asking for a donation at the door.

Free The Children also has many ideas for larger groups like schools or communities. One idea is to get

Providing services, participating in an "athon," and holding specific events are Free The Children fundraising ideas that young people can participate in.

people involved in an "athon" For these events, participants sign up **sponsors.** Sponsors are people or organizations who make pledges. Some ideas include runathons, danceathons, and singathons. Another popular fundraiser is to sell something that students can have delivered to each other, like a candygram. Other ideas include holding events like spelling bees, benefit concerts, raffles, and carnivals.

Fundraisers are also a great way to educate people about what the funds will be used for. Participants can make posters to display, distribute informational brochures, and talk to people about their cause.

Raise Awareness

Teaching other people about the issue is an important part of eliminating child labor. People in wealthy countries often do not know that many of the products they purchase are made by children. Free The Children offers a great deal of information about child labor, education, and other problems that children in developing countries face.

Free The Children also offers help for young people who want to improve their public speaking skills. They provide step-by-step instructions on how to write and give a powerful and interesting speech. Young people who want to focus on raising awareness of social issues through public speaking can join Free The Children's Youth Speakers Bureau.

Me to We

Craig has done a great deal of public speaking in his work with Free The Children and Leaders Today. In 2006 Craig and his brother, Marc, wrote a book called *Me to We: Finding Meaning in a Material World*. This book is a collection of stories and ideas meant to inspire personal and social change. According to the Me to We Web site:

At the most basic level, it embraces the idea that we can all build a better life—and our ideal world—through reaching out to others. In practice, it involves focusing less on "Me," and more on "We"—our communities, our nation and our world as a whole.[15]

Both the *Me to We* book and Web site offer ideas for ways to make a difference every day. All of the money made from selling the book goes to support Free The Children.

Craig, left, and Marc started Me to We and wrote a book called *Me to We: Finding Meaning in a Material World.* Me to We is meant to inspire people to make a difference.

Today, Craig is in his mid-twenties, but he still works to help improve the lives of others.

Craig Today

Between his many speaking engagements and trips to developing countries, Craig still managed to earn a degree in peace and conflict resolution from the University of Toronto in 2006. Now in his mid-twenties, he is still enthusiastic about his cause. Craig continues to work to improve the lives of disadvantaged people throughout the world and to encourage others to do the same. "Through one small meaningful action after another, any of us can change the world,"[16] says Craig.

Notes

Chapter One: Inspired to Help

1. Craig Kielburger with Kevin Major, *Free the Children: A Young Man's Personal Crusade Against Child Labor*. New York: Harper-Collins, 1998, p. 17.

2. Quoted in "A Voice for the Children," *Kiwanis*, June–July 2004.

3. Kielburger, *Free the Children*, p. 10.

4. Craig Kielburger, "Kids Can Free the Children," www.freethechildren.com/pressroom/source/publications/Chicken%20Soup%20for%20the%20Canadian%20Soul%202002%20Craig%20Kielburger.pdf.

Chapter Two: Off to Asia

5. Craig and Marc Kielburger, *Me to We: Finding Meaning in a Material World*. New York: Fireside Books, 2006, p. 7.

6. Craig and Marc Kielburger, "Finding Purpose Through the Power of Our Own Contributions," www.freethechildren.com/pressroom/source/publications/Essay%20for%20Power%20of%20Purpose.pdf.

7. Kielburger, "Kids Can Free the Children."

8. Kielburger, *Free the Children*, p. 164.

9. Kielburger, *Free the Children* p. 165.

10. Kielburger, *Free the Children*, p. 193.

Chapter Three: Free The Children in Action

11. Craig Kielburger, testimony in the Democratic Policy Committee hearing on Consumer Choice and Corporate Responsibility, April 29, 1996. Reprinted by *Human Rights for Workers*, www.senser.com/ftctalk.htm.

12. Leaders Today. http://leaderstoday.com/aboutus/history.php.

13. Free The Children, School Building FAQ. www.freethechildren.com/programs/schoolbuilding/schoolbuilding_schoolbuildingfaq.htm.

Chapter Four: What You Can Do

14. Free The Children, Halloween for Hunger Campaign, www.freethechildren.com/we/halloweenforhunger/docs/H4H_1pager.pdf.

15. Me to We, "Me to We Philosophy," www.metowe.org/about/me-to-we-philosophy.html.

16. Quoted in "Behind Each Problem, Issue and Statistic There Is a Human Life," *Citizen's Weekly*, November 27, 2005, www.enfantsentraide.org/ftc/source/news/2005/The_Ottawa_Citizen_nov27_05_BehindEachProblem.pdf.

Glossary

activist: A person who takes action to bring about change.

developing countries: Poor countries that are becoming more advanced.

honorary doctorates: Degrees given by a university to an individual as an honor rather than because he or she completed the required classes.

lobbying: Attempting to influence the decisions of government officials.

negotiating: Participating in discussions with an opposing party in order to come to an agreement.

nonprofit organization: An organization that does not operate to make a profit, but rather to support a cause such as a school or charity.

petition: A document signed by many people demanding an action from the government or other authority.

pledged: Promised to donate money to a charitable cause.

poverty: The state of being extremely poor.

press conference: A meeting at which a government official or a celebrity makes an announcement to members of the press, who ask questions.

prime minister: The head of an elected government, similar to the president of the United States.

rehabilitation center: A place where people stay for a period of time to recover from a traumatic experience before reentering society.

slums: Areas of a city where people live in poverty.

sponsors: People who give money to charity to fund a specific event.

standing ovation: When a seated audience stands and applauds an exceptional performance.

syringes: Medical devices used for injecting or withdrawing fluids from the body.

For Further Exploration

Books

Rob Bowden, *World Poverty*. Chicago: Raintree, 2003. This book discusses poverty around the world, giving real-life examples. Includes color photographs and a glossary.

Sondra Clark, *You Can Change Your World! Creative Ways to Volunteer and Make a Difference*. Grand Rapids, MI: Revell, 2003. This book, written by a thirteen-year-old, offers 150 ways for kids to make the world a better place.

Craig Kielburger with Kevin Major, *Free the Children: A Young Man's Personal Crusade Against Child Labor*. New York: HarperCollins, 1998. In this book, Craig tells the exciting story of his first trip to Asia.

Barbara A. Lewis, *The Kid's Guide to Social Action: How to Solve the Social Problems You Choose—and Turn Creative Thinking into Positive Action*. Minneapolis: Free Spirit, 1998. This book gives step-by-step instructions on ways to get involved in social action. Also includes stories of kids and teens who made a difference.

Jennifer Reed, *Elizabeth Bloomer: Child Labor Activist*. Detroit: KidHaven Press, 2006. This book, also in the Young Heroes series, tells the story of Elizabeth Bloomer, another young person who was influenced by the life and work of Iqbal Masih.

Web Sites

DO Something (www.dosomething.org). This Web site encourages young people to make positive changes in the world. It includes information on how to get involved and on what other young people are doing.

Free The Children (www.freethechildren.com/index. php). The Free The Children Web site is an amazing resource for young people who want to make a difference in the world. In addition to information about Craig and Free The Children's programs, the site offers a wealth of resources on child labor, fundraising, and public speaking.

Unite for Children (www.unicef.org). This site offers information about United Nations Children's Fund (UNICEF) programs around the world.

The World's Children's Prize for the Rights of the Child 2000: Iqbal Masih (www.childrensworld.org/global classroom/page.html?pid=53). This site tells Iqbal's story with vivid details and photos.

Index

Picture Credits

Cover photo: AP Images
AP Images, 8, 12, 20
Photo Courtesy of Free The Children, 5, 7, 10,
    11, 15, 17, 23, 25, 28, 31, 32, 35
Photo Courtesy of Free The Children,
    photographed by Colin Corneau, 38
Photo Courtesy of Free The Children,
    photographed by Scott Ramsay, 37

About the Author

Rachel Lynette has written over 25 books for children as well as many articles on children and family life. She has found the books of the Young Heroes series to be some of her most rewarding and enjoyable projects. She also teaches science to children of all ages. Rachel lives in the Seattle, Washington, area in the Songaia Cohousing Community with her two delightful children, David and Lucy; a cat named Cosette; and a playful white rat. When she is not teaching or writing, Rachel enjoys spending time with her family and friends, traveling, reading, drawing, inline skating, crocheting socks, and eating chocolate ice cream.